# TABLE OF CONTENTS

1. Introduction to Autism..................................................................................4
   - Definition and explanation of autism................................................5
   - Prevalence of autism..........................................................................5
   - History of autism................................................................................6
2. Symptoms of Autism......................................................................................7
   - Common behaviors and characteristics associated with autism.....7
   - How symptoms may vary from person to person.............................8
3. Causes of Autism..........................................................................................10
   - Genetic factors...................................................................................10
   - Environmental factors......................................................................11
   - Current research on causes of autism.............................................13
4. Diagnosing Autism.......................................................................................13
   - Evaluation process............................................................................14
   - Different types of professionals involved in diagnosis...................15
   - How to get a diagnosis for someone with autism............................15
5. Treatments and Interventions for Autism................................................17
   - Overview of available treatments and interventions.....................17
   - How to choose the right treatment or intervention for someone with autism..................................................................................................18
   - The role of therapy, medication, and other supports....................19
6. Living with Autism......................................................................................20
   - Strategies for managing daily life with autism...............................20
   - Support systems and resources for individuals with autism and their families..............................................................................................21
   - Advocacy and self-advocacy for people with autism.....................24
7. Conclusion....................................................................................................25

- **Summary of key points**......................................................................25
- **Role Models and Inspiration**..............................................................26
- **Encouragement for individuals with autism and their families**................27

# 1- Introduction to Autism

Welcome to our book on autism! In this book, we will explore the complex and often misunderstood disorder known as autism spectrum disorder (ASD). We will provide an overview of what autism is, how it is diagnosed, and the various treatments and interventions that are available to individuals with autism and their families.

Autism is a neurological disorder that affects communication and social interaction. It is characterized by difficulties with social communication and social interaction, and by restricted and repetitive patterns of behavior, interests, or activities. It is a spectrum disorder, which means that the severity of symptoms can vary greatly from one person to another. Some individuals with autism may be highly independent and able to live and work independently, while others may need significant support with daily living skills and may be nonverbal.

Despite its prevalence and increasing awareness, there is still a lot of misinformation and misunderstanding about autism. In this book, we aim to provide a clear and accurate introduction to the disorder, as well as practical information and resources for individuals with autism and their families. We will cover topics such as the symptoms of autism, the causes and risk factors for the disorder, and the evaluation and diagnostic process. We will also delve into the various treatments and interventions that are available, including therapy, medication, and other supports, and how to choose the right treatment plan for an individual with autism.

In addition to providing information on the disorder itself, we will also explore the challenges and joys of living with autism, and offer strategies and resources for managing daily life and advocating for oneself or a loved one with autism.

We hope that this book will serve as a helpful and informative resource for anyone seeking to learn more about autism, whether you are a parent or caregiver, a professional working with individuals with autism, or someone with autism seeking to better understand and navigate your own experience. So, let's get started on this journey of understanding and exploring the world of autism together.

- **Definition and explanation of autism**

Autism, also known as autism spectrum disorder (ASD), is a complex neurodevelopmental disorder that affects communication and social interaction. It is characterized by difficulties with social communication and social interaction, and by restricted and repetitive patterns of behavior, interests, or activities.

People with autism may have difficulty with social interaction, such as making eye contact, initiating or maintaining conversations, or understanding social cues and body language. They may also have difficulty with verbal and nonverbal communication, such as speaking, using gestures, or interpreting the speech and facial expressions of others.

Restricted and repetitive patterns of behavior, interests, or activities are also common in individuals with autism. This may include repetitive movements or routines, a need for strict routine or consistency, and a strong interest in specific topics or objects.

Autism is a spectrum disorder, which means that the severity of symptoms can vary greatly from one person to another. Some individuals with autism may be highly independent and able to live and work independently, while others may need significant support with daily living skills and may be nonverbal.

Autism is not a mental illness or a result of poor parenting. It is a neurological disorder that is present from birth or early childhood, and it is caused by a combination of genetic and environmental factors. There is currently no cure for autism, but early intervention and treatment can greatly improve outcomes for individuals with autism.

- **Prevalence of autism**

The prevalence of autism varies widely around the world, with some studies reporting higher prevalence rates and others reporting lower rates.

According to a recent report by the World Health Organization (WHO), the global prevalence of autism is estimated to be around 1% of the population. However, the WHO notes that the true prevalence of autism may be higher, as many cases may go undiagnosed or misdiagnosed in low- and middle-income countries.

The prevalence of autism may also vary within different countries and regions. For example, some studies have found higher rates of autism in developed countries compared to developing countries, although this may be influenced by factors such as diagnostic practices, access to services, and cultural differences.

It is important to note that the prevalence of autism is a complex issue and more research is needed to fully understand the factors that contribute to its occurrence. Factors that may influence the prevalence of autism include genetic and environmental factors, as well as diagnostic practices and access to services.

According to the Centers for Disease Control and Prevention (CDC), autism affects an estimated 1 in 54 children in the United States. This means that approximately 1.7% of children in the U.S. have been diagnosed with autism.

Autism is more common in boys than girls, with a ratio of about 4:1. However, it is important to note that this ratio may be influenced by factors such as diagnostic bias and the fact that girls may be more likely to go undiagnosed due to differing symptom presentation.

The prevalence of autism has increased significantly in recent years. According to the CDC, the prevalence of autism in the U.S. has more than tripled since 2000, when it was estimated to affect 1 in 150 children. This increase may be due to a combination of factors, including improved awareness and identification of the disorder, changes in diagnostic criteria, and increased access to services.

It is important to note that the prevalence of autism may vary widely depending on the population being studied and the criteria used to define the disorder. Some studies have reported higher prevalence rates, while others have reported lower rates.

Overall, the prevalence of autism is an important public health concern and efforts are needed to improve awareness, diagnosis, and treatment of the disorder globally.

- **History of autism**

The history of autism is long and complex, with descriptions of symptoms and behaviors similar to those of autism dating back to ancient times. However, the term "autism" was not coined until the early 20th century.

In the early 1900s, a Swiss psychiatrist named Eugene Bleuler used the term "autism" to describe the social withdrawal and isolated thinking that he observed in some of his patients with schizophrenia. The term "autism" comes from the Greek word "autos," meaning "self," and was meant to describe the inward-looking and self-absorbed nature of these individuals.

In 1943, Austrian psychiatrist Leo Kanner published a paper describing 11 children with similar symptoms of social withdrawal and difficulty with communication and social interaction. Kanner referred to this condition as "early infantile autism," and his work is often considered the first formal description of the disorder.

In the 1950s and 1960s, another psychiatrist, Bruno Bettelheim, popularized the theory that autism was caused by "refrigerator mothers" who were emotionally cold and distant towards their children. This theory was later discredited and is now considered to be harmful and misleading.

In the 1980s, the diagnostic criteria for autism were revised and expanded to include a wider range of symptoms and behaviors, and the disorder was renamed "autism spectrum disorder" to reflect the wide range of severity and symptoms that can be present in individuals with autism.

Today, autism is widely recognized as a complex neurodevelopmental disorder that is caused by a combination of genetic and environmental factors. Research on the causes, diagnosis, and treatment of autism continues to evolve, and there is ongoing debate and discussion about the best approaches to support individuals with autism and their families.

# 2- Symptoms of Autism

In this chapter, we will delve into the intricate world of symptoms that characterize autism spectrum disorder. From common behaviors that define the condition to the remarkable diversity in how these symptoms manifest from person to person, we'll uncover the essential elements that shape the autism experience. Let's begin by delving into the familiar behaviors and characteristics that are often associated with autism.

- **Common behaviors and characteristics associated with autism**

Here are some common behaviors and characteristics that are often associated with autism:

1. Social communication and interaction: Individuals with autism may have difficulty with social interaction, such as making eye contact, initiating or maintaining conversations, or understanding social cues and body language. They may also have difficulty with verbal and nonverbal communication, such as speaking, using gestures, or interpreting the speech and facial expressions of others.

2. Restricted and repetitive behaviors: Individuals with autism may engage in repetitive movements or routines, have a need for strict routine or consistency, or have a strong interest in specific topics or objects. This may include repetitive behaviors such as hand-flapping or rocking, or a need to follow the same routine or order each day.

3. Sensory processing issues: Some individuals with autism may have difficulty processing sensory information, such as sights, sounds, or touch. They may be oversensitive or under-sensitive to certain stimuli, or may have difficulty interpreting or reacting to sensory information in an appropriate way.

4. Difficulty with flexibility and change: Many individuals with autism have difficulty adapting to change or new situations. They may struggle with transitions or with unexpected changes in their routine or environment.

5. Difficulty with social and emotional regulation: Individuals with autism may have difficulty expressing and interpreting emotions, and may have difficulty regulating their own emotions. They may also have difficulty understanding the emotions of others.

6. Unusual interests or fixations: Some individuals with autism may have unusually strong or specific interests, such as a particular topic or object. They may spend a lot of time learning about or engaging with their interest, and may have a hard time diverting their attention from it.

7. Difficulty with pretend play: Many children with autism have difficulty engaging in pretend play, which is a normal part of child development. They may have trouble understanding the concept of pretend and may not engage in imaginative play with toys or other objects.
8. Unusual sensory seeking or avoidance behaviors: Some individuals with autism may seek out certain sensory experiences, such as certain sounds or textures, or may avoid certain stimuli due to oversensitivity or under-sensitivity.
9. Difficulty with executive functioning skills: Executive functioning skills refer to the cognitive processes that allow us to plan, organize, and execute tasks. Some individuals with autism may have difficulty with these skills, which can affect their ability to complete tasks and make decisions.
10. Intellectual or developmental delays: Some individuals with autism may have intellectual or developmental delays, such as difficulty with language or cognitive skills. These delays may be mild or severe, and may vary from one individual to another.
11. Unusual play with toys or objects: Some individuals with autism may engage in unusual or repetitive play with toys or objects, such as lining them up or spinning them repeatedly. They may also have difficulty using toys in a typical or imaginative way.
12. Difficulty with social reciprocity: Social reciprocity refers to the ability to take turns and interact with others in a back-and-forth manner. Some individuals with autism may have difficulty with social reciprocity, such as initiating or responding to social interactions or engaging in turn-taking activities.
13. Unusual sensory interests: Some individuals with autism may have unusual sensory interests, such as an intense interest in certain textures or sounds. They may seek out sensory experiences or engage in repetitive sensory-seeking behaviors.
14. Unusual speech patterns: Some individuals with autism may have unusual speech patterns, such as speaking in a monotone or speaking with a peculiar inflection. They may also have difficulty initiating or maintaining conversations or may have delays in language development.
15. Unusual social behaviors: Some individuals with autism may exhibit unusual social behaviors, such as avoiding eye contact or having difficulty understanding personal space. They may also have difficulty understanding or expressing social cues or body language.

It is important to note that these behaviors and characteristics are not exhaustive, and that every individual with autism is unique and may exhibit a wide range of symptoms and behaviors. It is also important to remember that individuals with autism can and do learn and grow throughout their lives, and that with the right support and interventions, they can make significant progress and achieve their full potential.

- **How symptoms may vary from person to person**

Autism is characterized by difficulties with social communication and social interaction, and by restricted and repetitive patterns of behavior, interests, or activities.

Symptoms of ASD can vary greatly from one person to another, both in terms of the type and severity of symptoms present. Some individuals with ASD may have mild symptoms and be highly independent, while others may have severe symptoms and need significant support with daily living skills.

Here are some factors that may contribute to the variation in symptoms among individuals with ASD:

1. Age of diagnosis: Symptoms of ASD may become more noticeable as a child grows and develops, and an early diagnosis may lead to earlier intervention and treatment. As a result, individuals who are diagnosed at a younger age may have milder symptoms and a better prognosis than those who are diagnosed later in life.

2. Severity of symptoms: Symptoms of ASD can range from mild to severe, and the severity of symptoms may influence an individual's ability to function independently. For example, an individual with mild symptoms may be able to live and work independently, while an individual with severe symptoms may need significant support with daily living skills and may be nonverbal.

3. Comorbid conditions: Some individuals with ASD may also have other medical or mental health conditions, such as intellectual disability, epilepsy, or anxiety. These conditions may affect the severity and presentation of ASD symptoms.

4. Environmental factors: Environmental factors, such as access to education and supportive services, may also influence the severity and presentation of ASD symptoms.

5. Genetic factors: ASD is thought to be caused by a combination of genetic and environmental factors. Some individuals with ASD may have a family history of the disorder, while others may have no known genetic risk factors. The specific genetic mutations or variations that are associated with ASD may also vary from person to person, and may contribute to the variation in symptoms.

6. Neurodiversity: Some individuals with ASD may be part of the neurodiversity movement, which advocates for the recognition and acceptance of neurological differences as a natural part of human diversity. These individuals may view ASD as a natural part of their identity and may not see their symptoms as a disorder or deficit.

7. Coping strategies: Some individuals with ASD may develop coping strategies or accommodations that allow them to manage their symptoms and function more effectively in daily life. These strategies may vary from person to person and may contribute to the variation in symptoms.

8. Support and interventions: The type and intensity of support and interventions that an individual with ASD receives may also influence their symptoms and functional abilities. Early and intensive interventions, such as therapy and educational support,

may help individuals with ASD make significant progress and achieve their full potential.

# 3- Causes of Autism

The exact cause of autism is not yet known, but researchers believe that it is caused by a combination of genetic and environmental factors. This means that both a person's genes and their environment may play a role in the development of autism.

Genetic factors refer to the inherited characteristics that a person gets from their parents. Some people with autism may have a family history of the condition, which suggests that genetics may play a role in its development.

Environmental factors refer to the surroundings and conditions in which a person lives. These may include things like exposure to certain toxins or infections during pregnancy, or other stressors or influences that may affect the development of the brain.

Researchers are still studying the causes of autism and how different factors may interact to contribute to its development. It is important to note that autism is not caused by a single gene or environmental factor, but rather by a complex interplay of multiple factors.

Overall, understanding the causes of autism is an important step towards improving diagnosis and treatment of the disorder, and towards supporting individuals with autism and their families.

- **Genetic factors**

Genetic factors are inherited characteristics that are passed down from a person's parents. Research has shown that genetics play a role in the development of autism, although the specific genetic mutations or variations that are associated with the disorder are not yet fully understood.

Here are some key points about the genetic factors of autism:

1. Multiple genes are involved: It is thought that multiple genes are involved in the development of autism, and that these genes may interact with each other and with environmental factors in complex ways. Some studies have identified specific genetic mutations or variations that are associated with ASD, while others have found that common genetic variations may increase the risk of ASD.

2. Inheritance patterns are complex: The inheritance patterns of ASD are complex and may vary from one family to another. In some cases, ASD may be inherited in a straightforward manner, with a clear pattern of transmission from parent to child. In other cases, ASD may be caused by a combination of genetic and environmental factors, or may be the result of a spontaneous genetic mutation that is not inherited from a person's parents.

3. Genetic testing is available: Genetic testing is available for ASD, and may be used to identify specific genetic mutations or variations that are associated with the disorder. Genetic testing may be helpful in diagnosing ASD, predicting an individual's risk of developing the disorder, and guiding treatment and management decisions.
4. Genetic factors are not the only cause of ASD: It is important to note that genetics are not the only cause of ASD, and that the disorder is likely caused by a complex interplay of multiple genetic and environmental factors.
5. Family studies: Family studies are a type of research that involves examining the occurrence of a condition in families to identify genetic and environmental factors that may contribute to the development of the condition. Some family studies have found that ASD is more common among siblings of individuals with ASD, suggesting a genetic component to the disorder.
6. Twin studies: Twin studies are a type of research that compares the occurrence of a condition in identical (monozygotic) twins, who share the same genetic makeup, to the occurrence of the condition in non-identical (dizygotic) twins, who share only about half of their genetic material. Some twin studies have found that the concordance rate (the likelihood that both twins will have the condition) is higher for monozygotic twins than for dizygotic twins, suggesting a genetic component to ASD.
7. Genetic syndromes: Some genetic syndromes, such as Fragile X syndrome and tuberous sclerosis, are associated with an increased risk of ASD. These syndromes are caused by specific genetic mutations that are inherited in a predictable pattern.
8. Genetic testing: Genetic testing is a type of medical test that is used to identify specific genetic mutations or variations that may be associated with ASD. Genetic testing may be performed using a sample of an individual's DNA, which may be obtained through a blood sample or a saliva sample. Genetic testing may be helpful in diagnosing ASD, predicting an individual's risk of developing the disorder, and guiding treatment and management decisions.

Overall, the genetic factors of ASD are an important area of research, and more research is needed to fully understand the role of genetics in the development of the disorder. This knowledge may help to improve diagnosis and treatment of ASD, and may also provide insight into the underlying mechanisms of the disorder.

- **Environmental factors**

Environmental factors refer to the surroundings and conditions in which a person lives, and may include things like diet, toxins, infections, and other stressors or influences that may affect the development of the brain. Research has shown that environmental factors may play a role in the development of autism, although the specific environmental factors that are associated with the disorder are not yet fully understood.

Here are some key points about the environmental factors of autism:

1. Multiple environmental factors may be involved: It is thought that multiple environmental factors may be involved in the development of autism, and that these factors may interact with each other and with genetic factors in complex ways. Some

studies have identified specific environmental factors, such as exposure to certain toxins or infections during pregnancy, that may increase the risk of ASD.

2. The timing of exposure may be important: The timing of exposure to environmental factors may be important in the development of ASD. For example, some studies have found that exposure to certain toxins or infections during critical periods of fetal brain development may increase the risk of ASD.

3. The role of epigenetic factors: Epigenetic factors refer to changes in gene expression that are not caused by changes in the underlying DNA sequence. Epigenetic changes may be influenced by environmental factors, such as diet, stress, or exposure to toxins, and may affect the development of ASD.

4. Environmental factors are not the only cause of ASD: It is important to note that environmental factors are not the only cause of ASD, and that the disorder is likely caused by a complex interplay of multiple genetic and environmental factors.

5. Prenatal and perinatal risk factors: Prenatal and perinatal risk factors are environmental factors that are present during pregnancy and the period immediately after birth. Some studies have found that certain prenatal and perinatal risk factors, such as exposure to certain toxins or infections during pregnancy, may increase the risk of ASD.

6. Maternal health conditions: Maternal health conditions, such as diabetes, epilepsy, and autoimmune disorders, may also increase the risk of ASD. It is not yet clear how these conditions may affect the development of the disorder, but some research suggests that they may influence the epigenetic regulation of gene expression or alter the immune system in a way that affects brain development.

7. Socioeconomic status: Some studies have found that children from lower socioeconomic backgrounds may be at an increased risk of ASD, although it is not yet clear how socioeconomic status may affect the development of the disorder.

8. Environmental toxins: Exposure to certain toxins, such as pesticides, heavy metals, and air pollution, has been linked to an increased risk of ASD. It is not yet clear how these toxins may affect the development of the disorder, but some research suggests that they may alter the epigenetic regulation of gene expression or disrupt the immune system in a way that affects brain development.

Overall, the environmental factors of ASD are an important area of research, and more research is needed to fully understand the role of the environment in the development of the disorder. This knowledge may help to improve diagnosis and treatment of ASD, and may also provide insight into the underlying mechanisms of the disorder.

- **Current research on causes of autism**

The exact causes of ASD are not fully understood, but research suggests that it is caused by a combination of genetic and environmental factors.

Here is an overview of some current research on the causes of autism:

1. Genetics: Researchers are studying the genetic factors that may contribute to the development of ASD. Some studies have identified specific genetic mutations or variations that are associated with ASD, such as mutations in the SHANK3 gene or the MECP2 gene. Other studies have found that common genetic variations, such as single nucleotide polymorphisms (SNPs) or copy number variations (CNVs), may increase the risk of ASD. Researchers are also exploring the role of epigenetic factors, such as DNA methylation or histone modification, which may be influenced by environmental exposures and may affect the development of ASD.

2. Environmental factors: Researchers are studying the environmental factors that may contribute to the development of ASD. Some studies have identified specific environmental exposures, such as exposure to certain toxins or infections during pregnancy, that may increase the risk of ASD. Other research is focusing on the role of epigenetic factors, which may be influenced by environmental exposures and may affect the development of ASD.

3. Developmental processes: Researchers are studying the developmental processes that may be disrupted in individuals with ASD, such as brain development, neural connectivity, and immune system function. This research may provide insight into the underlying mechanisms of ASD and may lead to the development of new treatments and interventions.

4. Animal models: Researchers are using animal models, such as mice or zebrafish, to study the genetic and environmental factors that may contribute to the development of ASD. These models may help researchers to understand the underlying mechanisms of the disorder and to identify potential therapeutic targets.

## 4- Diagnosing Autism

If you suspect that you or someone you know may have ASD, it is important to seek a proper evaluation and diagnosis from a qualified healthcare provider.

The process of diagnosing ASD typically involves a thorough evaluation by a team of healthcare professionals, including doctors, psychologists, and speech therapists. The evaluation may include a physical examination, a review of the individual's medical history and developmental history, and assessments of the individual's communication and social skills.

There are no specific medical tests for ASD, and the diagnosis is typically made based on a combination of observation, evaluation, and input from caregivers and family members.

The process of diagnosing ASD may take some time and may involve multiple visits to a healthcare provider.

- **Evaluation process**

The evaluation process for autism spectrum disorder (ASD), typically involves a thorough evaluation by a team of healthcare professionals, including doctors, psychologists, and speech therapists. The evaluation may include a physical examination, a review of the individual's medical history and developmental history, and assessments of the individual's communication and social skills.

Here is an overview of the evaluation process for ASD:

1. Physical examination: The healthcare provider will perform a physical examination to assess the individual's overall health and to rule out any medical conditions that may be causing the individual's symptoms.
2. Review of medical and developmental history: The healthcare provider will review the individual's medical history, including any prenatal and perinatal risk factors that may be associated with ASD, as well as the individual's developmental history. This may include information about the individual's milestones, such as when they began to crawl, walk, or talk.
3. Assessments of communication and social skills: The healthcare provider will assess the individual's communication and social skills to determine if they meet the criteria for ASD. This may include assessments of the individual's language and speech development, their ability to make eye contact and engage in social interactions, and their ability to understand and respond to social cues.
4. Input from caregivers and family members: The healthcare provider will also consider input from caregivers and family members, as they may have valuable insights into the individual's development and behavior.
5. Diagnostic criteria: The healthcare provider will use diagnostic criteria from the Diagnostic and Statistical Manual of Mental Disorders (DSM) or the International Classification of Diseases (ICD) to determine if the individual meets the criteria for ASD. These criteria include specific behaviors and characteristics that are commonly associated with ASD, such as difficulty with social interaction and communication, repetitive behaviors, and narrow or restricted interests.
6. Differential diagnosis: The healthcare provider will also consider other conditions that may have similar symptoms to ASD, such as intellectual disability, language delays, or attention deficit hyperactivity disorder (ADHD). It is important to properly diagnose any underlying conditions in order to provide appropriate treatment and support.
7. Referral to specialists: If the healthcare provider suspects that the individual may have ASD, they may refer the individual to a specialist, such as a developmental pediatrician or a psychologist, for further evaluation. The specialist may use additional assessment tools or techniques to confirm the diagnosis.

8. Ongoing evaluation and monitoring: The process of diagnosing ASD is ongoing, and the individual may need to be reevaluated periodically to monitor their progress and to adjust their treatment and support as needed.

It is important to note that the process of evaluating and diagnosing ASD may take some time, and it is important to be patient and to work closely with the healthcare team to ensure that the individual receives the appropriate evaluation and treatment.

- **Different types of professionals involved in diagnosis**

The process of diagnosing autism, typically involves a team of healthcare professionals, including doctors, psychologists, and speech therapists. Each of these professionals plays a specific role in the evaluation and diagnosis process.

Here is an overview of the different types of professionals involved in the diagnosis of ASD:

1. Doctors: Doctors, such as pediatricians or family doctors, are responsible for performing physical examinations and reviewing the individual's medical history. They may also order certain medical tests, such as blood tests or imaging studies, to rule out other conditions that may be causing the individual's symptoms.

2. Psychologists: Psychologists are trained in the assessment of mental health conditions, including ASD. They may use a variety of assessment tools and techniques, such as standardized tests or structured interviews, to evaluate the individual's communication and social skills.
3. Speech therapists: Speech therapists, also known as speech-language pathologists, are trained in the assessment and treatment of communication and language disorders. They may assess the individual's language and speech development and provide therapy to help improve these skills.
4. Developmental pediatricians: Developmental pediatricians are doctors who specialize in the evaluation and treatment of developmental disorders, including ASD. They may provide a comprehensive evaluation of the individual's development and may provide recommendations for treatment and support.
5. Other professionals: Depending on the individual's needs and the resources available, the diagnosis and evaluation team may also include other professionals, such as occupational therapists, behavior analysts, or social workers.

Overall, it is important to work closely with the healthcare team to ensure that the individual receives a thorough evaluation and receives the appropriate treatment and support.

- **How to get a diagnosis for someone with autism**

If you suspect that someone you know may have autism (ASD), it is important to seek a proper evaluation and diagnosis from a qualified healthcare provider. Getting a diagnosis can be a complex and time-consuming process, but it is an important step in ensuring that the individual receives the appropriate treatment and support.

Here is an overview of how to get a diagnosis for someone with ASD:

1. Talk to a healthcare provider: The first step in getting a diagnosis for ASD is to speak with a healthcare provider, such as a pediatrician or family doctor. They can assess the individual's overall health and discuss your concerns with you.

2. Request a referral to a specialist: If the healthcare provider suspects that the individual may have ASD, they may refer the individual to a specialist, such as a developmental pediatrician or a psychologist, for further evaluation.
3. Participate in the evaluation process: The evaluation process for ASD typically involves a thorough evaluation by a team of healthcare professionals, including doctors, psychologists, and speech therapists. The evaluation may include a physical examination, a review of the individual's medical history and developmental history, and assessments of the individual's communication and social skills. It is important to participate in this process and to provide as much information as possible about the individual's development and behavior.
4. Follow the treatment plan: If the individual is diagnosed with ASD, the healthcare team will work with you to develop a treatment plan that is tailored to the individual's needs. It is important to follow the treatment plan and to communicate with the healthcare team about any concerns or questions you may have.
5. Seek support: Getting a diagnosis for ASD can be overwhelming, and it is important to seek support from family, friends, and support groups. These resources can provide you with valuable information and support as you navigate the process of diagnosis and treatment.
6. Consider the age of the individual: The process of diagnosing ASD may be different for individuals of different ages. For example, the evaluation process for young children may focus more on developmental milestones and behaviors, while the evaluation process for older children and adults may focus more on language and communication skills.
7. Gather information and documentation: It can be helpful to gather information and documentation about the individual's development and behavior, such as developmental assessments, school reports, or records of therapy or treatment. This information can be valuable in helping the healthcare team to make a diagnosis.
8. Be patient: The process of diagnosing ASD can be time-consuming, and it may take multiple visits to a healthcare provider to complete the evaluation. It is important to be patient and to work closely with the healthcare team to ensure that the individual receives a thorough evaluation.
9. Seek second opinions: If you are not satisfied with the diagnosis or treatment plan, you may want to seek a second opinion from another healthcare provider. It is important to ensure that you are comfortable with the diagnosis and treatment plan and that you have confidence in the healthcare team.

10. Consider the individual's needs and preferences: It is important to consider the individual's needs and preferences when seeking a diagnosis and treatment for ASD. This may include taking into account their age, communication abilities, and any underlying medical conditions they may have.

## 5- Treatments and Interventions for Autism

In this Chapter, we delve into the realm of treatments and interventions for autism. In the following sections, we'll navigate through the array of options designed to support individuals on the spectrum. From gaining an overview of the available treatments to understanding how to select the most fitting approach for someone with autism, and exploring the roles played by therapies, medications, and various forms of support – our journey into the world of autism interventions is about to begin. Let's start by exploring the wide range of treatments and interventions that have become essential tools in this landscape.

- **Overview of available treatments and interventions**

There is no cure for ASD, but there are a variety of treatments and interventions that can help individuals with ASD to manage their symptoms and to improve their communication and social skills.

The most effective treatments and interventions for ASD are typically tailored to the individual's needs and may involve a combination of therapies, medications, and other interventions. It is important to work closely with a healthcare team to determine the most appropriate treatment plan for the individual.

Treatment and intervention options for ASD may include:

1. Behavioral therapies: Behavioral therapies, such as applied behavior analysis (ABA) or cognitive behavioral therapy (CBT), are widely used in the treatment of ASD. These therapies can help individuals with ASD to improve their communication and social skills, as well as to manage problem behaviors. Behavioral therapies often involve structured and systematic teaching methods, and may involve one-on-one sessions with a therapist or small group sessions.

2. Medications: Medications may be used to treat specific symptoms of ASD, such as anxiety, attention deficits, or repetitive behaviors. Some commonly used medications for ASD include stimulants, such as Ritalin or Adderall, which may be used to improve attention and focus; selective serotonin reuptake inhibitors (SSRIs), such as Prozac or Zoloft, which may be used to treat anxiety and depression; and antipsychotic medications, such as risperidone or aripiprazole, which may be used to treat severe problem behaviors. It is important to work closely with a healthcare provider to determine the most appropriate medication and dosage for the individual.

3. Educational and support services: Educational and support services, such as special education or speech therapy, can help individuals with ASD to learn new skills and to

better communicate with others. These services may be provided in a school setting or in a specialized therapy center, and may involve one-on-one or small group sessions with a therapist or educator.

4. Alternative and complementary therapies: Alternative and complementary therapies, such as dietary supplements or sensory integration therapy, may be used to complement traditional treatments. It is important to speak with a healthcare provider before starting any alternative or complementary therapies, as some of these therapies may have potential risks or may not be supported by scientific evidence.
5. Other interventions: Other interventions that may be helpful for individuals with ASD include assistive technology, such as communication devices or adaptive equipment, and social skills training, which can help individuals to learn and practice social skills in a structured and supportive environment.

Overall, the best treatment and intervention plan for ASD will depend on the individual's specific needs and circumstances, and it is important to work closely with a healthcare team to determine the most appropriate course of treatment.

- **How to choose the right treatment or intervention for someone with autism**

Choosing the right treatment or intervention for someone with autism, can be a complex and challenging process. There are a variety of treatment and intervention options available for ASD, and it is important to choose the one that is most appropriate for the individual's needs and circumstances.

Here are some tips for choosing the right treatment or intervention for someone with ASD:

1. Consult with a healthcare team: It is important to consult with a healthcare team, including doctors, psychologists, and other professionals, to determine the most appropriate treatment or intervention for the individual. The healthcare team can provide guidance and recommendations based on the individual's specific needs and circumstances.

2. Consider the individual's needs and preferences: It is important to consider the individual's needs and preferences when choosing a treatment or intervention. This may include taking into account their age, communication abilities, and any underlying medical conditions they may have.
3. Seek input from caregivers and family members: Caregivers and family members may have valuable insights into the individual's development and behavior, and it is important to seek their input when choosing a treatment or intervention.
4. Research the available options: It is important to research the available treatment and intervention options and to gather as much information as possible about their effectiveness and potential risks and benefits.
5. Be open to trying different interventions: It may take some time to find the treatment or intervention that is most effective for the individual, and it may be necessary to try different options before finding the one that works best. It is important to be open to

trying different interventions and to be patient as the individual adjusts to new treatment approaches.
6. Consider the individual's long-term goals: It is important to consider the individual's long-term goals when choosing a treatment or intervention. This may include goals related to communication, socialization, independence, or other areas of development.

7. Take into account the level of support needed: The level of support needed for the individual may vary depending on the treatment or intervention chosen. It is important to consider the amount of support and guidance the individual will need, as well as the availability of resources and support from caregivers and family members.
8. Evaluate the cost and accessibility of treatment options: The cost and accessibility of treatment options may be an important consideration when choosing a treatment or intervention. It is important to research the costs of different treatment options and to consider any financial assistance or insurance coverage that may be available.
9. Seek the advice of other families or individuals with ASD: It can be helpful to seek the advice of other families or individuals with ASD who have experience with different treatment and intervention options. They may be able to provide valuable insights and recommendations.
10. Be open to adjusting the treatment plan: It is important to be open to adjusting the treatment plan as needed, based on the individual's progress and changing needs. It may be necessary to modify the treatment plan or to try different interventions if the initial treatment is not effective.

Overall, choosing the right treatment or intervention for someone with ASD requires careful consideration and may involve trying different options before finding the one that works best. It is important to work closely with a healthcare team and to seek input from caregivers and family members to ensure that the individual receives the most appropriate treatment and support.

- **The role of therapy, medication, and other supports**

    Therapy, medication, and other supports can play a vital role in the treatment and management of autism. Here is an overview of the role of these interventions:

1. Therapy: Therapy can help individuals with ASD to improve their communication and social skills, as well as to manage problem behaviors. Behavioral therapies, such as applied behavior analysis (ABA) or cognitive behavioral therapy (CBT), are widely used in the treatment of ASD. These therapies may involve structured and systematic teaching methods, and may involve one-on-one sessions with a therapist or small group sessions. Other types of therapy that may be helpful for individuals with ASD include speech therapy, occupational therapy, and social skills training.

2. Medication: Medication may be used to treat specific symptoms of ASD, such as anxiety, attention deficits, or repetitive behaviors. Some commonly used medications for ASD include stimulants, such as Ritalin or Adderall, which may be used to improve attention and focus; selective serotonin reuptake inhibitors (SSRIs), such as Prozac or

Zoloft, which may be used to treat anxiety and depression; and antipsychotic medications, such as risperidone or aripiprazole, which may be used to treat severe problem behaviors. It is important to work closely with a healthcare provider to determine the most appropriate medication and dosage for the individual.

3. Other supports: Other supports that may be helpful for individuals with ASD include assistive technology, such as communication devices or adaptive equipment, and educational and support services, such as special education or speech therapy. These supports can help individuals with ASD to learn new skills and to better communicate with others.

# 6- Living with Autism

Step into Chapter 6, a realm dedicated to the intricate art of living with autism. Here, we'll journey through the practical landscape of daily life as experienced by individuals on the spectrum. From unveiling effective strategies for navigating each day, to uncovering the pillars of support and resources available for both individuals with autism and their families, and finally, delving into the empowering realm of advocacy and self-advocacy – this chapter offers a holistic exploration of the dynamic world of autism in everyday life.

- **Strategies for managing daily life with autism**

There are a variety of strategies that can be helpful for managing daily life with autism. Here are a few examples:

1. Establish a routine: Establishing a predictable routine can be helpful for individuals with ASD, as it can provide structure and reduce uncertainty. A routine may include regular schedules for meals, sleep, and activities, as well as visual schedules or calendars to help the individual understand and prepare for the day's events.

2. Use visual supports: Visual supports, such as pictures or videos, can be helpful for individuals with ASD who have difficulty understanding and processing verbal instructions. Visual supports can be used to communicate tasks or routines, or to provide information about events or activities.

3. Encourage independence: Encouraging independence can be an important part of managing daily life with ASD. This may involve teaching the individual skills such as dressing, grooming, or household chores, or providing opportunities for them to make choices and decisions.

4. Manage sensory issues: Some individuals with ASD may have sensitivity to certain stimuli, such as noise or light, or may have difficulty processing sensory information. Strategies for managing sensory issues may include using noise-cancelling headphones, providing a quiet space, or using sensory integration therapy.

5. Communicate clearly and consistently: Clear and consistent communication can be helpful for individuals with ASD, who may have difficulty understanding and interpreting

verbal and nonverbal cues. This may involve using simple and concrete language, avoiding idioms or figurative language, and providing visual supports when necessary.

6. Seek support: Seeking support from family, friends, and support groups can be an important part of managing daily life with ASD. Support from others can provide valuable information and resources, as well as emotional support and a sense of community.

- **Support systems and resources for individuals with autism and their families**

Support systems and resources for individuals with autism and their families can take many forms, depending on the specific needs and preferences of the individual with autism and their family. Some common types of support and resources include:

1. Educational support: Educational support for individuals with autism can take many forms and may vary depending on the specific needs and abilities of the individual. Some common types of educational support for individuals with autism include:

> - Special education programs: These are educational programs that are specifically designed for individuals with disabilities, including autism. Special education programs can be provided in public schools or through private schools or institutions. These programs often involve small class sizes, individualized instruction, and a focus on helping individuals with autism learn and grow at their own pace.
>
> - Inclusive education: This refers to the practice of educating individuals with autism in a regular classroom alongside their non-disabled peers. Inclusive education can be beneficial for individuals with autism as it allows them to learn and interact with their peers in a natural environment.
>
> - Applied behavior analysis (ABA): This is a type of therapy that is often used to teach new skills and behaviors to individuals with autism. ABA therapy involves breaking down tasks into small steps and using positive reinforcement to encourage desired behaviors.
>
> - Speech therapy: This type of therapy can help individuals with autism improve their communication skills and language development. Speech therapists may work with individuals on a one-to-one basis or in small groups.
>
> - Occupational therapy: Occupational therapy can help individuals with autism improve their fine motor skills, sensory processing, and overall functioning. Occupational therapists may use a variety of techniques, including sensory integration therapy, to help individuals with autism learn new skills and improve their abilities.
>
> - Overall, educational support for individuals with autism can be an important part of helping them learn and grow in a supportive and inclusive environment.

2. Behavioral and therapeutic support: Behavioral and therapeutic support for individuals with autism can take many forms and may vary depending on the specific needs and abilities of the individual. Some common types of behavioral and therapeutic support for individuals with autism include:

- Applied behavior analysis (ABA): This is a type of therapy that is often used to teach new skills and behaviors to individuals with autism. ABA therapy involves breaking down tasks into small steps and using positive reinforcement to encourage desired behaviors.

- Cognitive behavioral therapy (CBT): This type of therapy can help individuals with autism understand and change negative thought patterns and behaviors. CBT can be helpful in addressing issues such as anxiety, depression, and anger management.

- Speech therapy: This type of therapy can help individuals with autism improve their communication skills and language development. Speech therapists may work with individuals on a one-to-one basis or in small groups.

- Occupational therapy: Occupational therapy can help individuals with autism improve their fine motor skills, sensory processing, and overall functioning. Occupational therapists may use a variety of techniques, including sensory integration therapy, to help individuals with autism learn new skills and improve their abilities.

- Social skills training: This type of therapy can help individuals with autism learn and practice social skills, such as how to initiate conversations, how to read social cues, and how to make friends.

Overall, behavioral and therapeutic support can be an important part of helping individuals with autism improve their communication skills, social skills, and overall functioning. It is important to work with a qualified therapist or professional to determine the best course of treatment for an individual with autism.

3. Medical support: Medical support for individuals with autism can be an important part of helping them manage any medical conditions they may have and maintain good overall health. Some common types of medical support for individuals with autism include:

- Primary care: Individuals with autism may see a primary care provider, such as a pediatrician or family doctor, for regular check-ups and to manage any medical conditions.

- Specialists: Depending on the needs of the individual with autism, they may see specialists such as neurologists, gastroenterologists, or endocrinologists to manage specific medical conditions.

- Medications: Some individuals with autism may take medications to manage medical conditions or to address behaviors that may be challenging. It is important to work closely with a healthcare provider to determine the appropriate medications and dosages for an individual with autism.

- Alternative therapies: Some individuals with autism and their families may choose to pursue alternative therapies, such as dietary changes or supplements, to help manage their symptoms. It is important to speak with a healthcare provider before starting any new treatment or therapy.

Overall, it is important for individuals with autism to have access to medical support that meets their needs and helps them maintain good overall health.

4. Social support : Social support for individuals with autism and their families can take many forms and can be an important part of helping individuals with autism feel connected and included in their communities. Some common types of social support for individuals with autism include:

- Support groups: Support groups are a great way for individuals with autism and their families to connect with others who are going through similar experiences. Support groups can provide a sense of community and offer a safe space to share experiences, ask questions, and get support.

- Online communities: There are many online communities, forums, and social media groups specifically for individuals with autism and their families. These can be a great way to connect with others, share information and resources, and get support.

- In-person events: Many communities and organizations host in-person events, such as picnics, festivals, and workshops, specifically for individuals with autism and their families. These events can provide an opportunity for individuals with autism and their families to connect with others and participate in fun and meaningful activities.

- Peer support: Some individuals with autism may benefit from connecting with other individuals with autism who can offer peer support and understanding. This can be especially helpful for older individuals with autism who may be looking for support and guidance from others who have similar experiences.

Overall, social support can be an important part of helping individuals with autism feel connected, included, and supported in their communities.

Financial support : Financial support for individuals with autism and their families can be an important part of helping them access the resources and support they need. Some common types of financial support for individuals with autism include:

- Government programs: There are a variety of government programs that can provide financial assistance to individuals with autism and their families. These programs may include Medicaid, Supplemental Security Income (SSI), and the Children's Health Insurance Program (CHIP).

- Grants and scholarships: There are a number of grants and scholarships available specifically for individuals with autism and their families. These may be offered by government agencies, nonprofit organizations, or private foundations.

- Private insurance: Many private insurance plans cover some or all of the costs of treatments and therapies for individuals with autism. It is important to check with an insurance provider to see what is covered under an individual's specific plan.

- Fundraising: Some individuals with autism and their families may choose to fundraise to cover the costs of treatments, therapies, and other expenses. There are a variety of ways to fundraise, including online crowdfunding platforms, community events, and personal fundraising efforts.

Overall, financial support can be an important part of helping individuals with autism and their families access the resources and support they need. It is important to explore all available options and to work with a financial planner or other professional to determine the best course of action.

- **Advocacy and self-advocacy for people with autism**
Advocacy and self-advocacy are important for individuals with autism and any other disability to ensure that their needs and rights are respected and supported.
Advocacy for individuals with autism can be carried out by a variety of people, including family members, friends, professionals, and advocates who are not themselves autistic. Advocacy can involve speaking up for the rights and needs of individuals with autism in various settings, such as schools, workplaces, and the community. This can involve writing letters, making phone calls, attending meetings, and participating in advocacy organizations.
Advocacy can be especially important for individuals with autism in situations where they may not be able to advocate for themselves. For example, a parent or advocate may speak up on behalf of a child with autism in a school setting to ensure that the child's needs are being met. Advocacy can also involve working to raise awareness about autism and the challenges that individuals with autism and their families may face.
Self-advocacy, on the other hand, is the act of speaking up for one's own needs and rights. This is an important skill for individuals with autism to develop as they grow and become more independent. Self-advocacy can involve learning how to communicate one's own needs and preferences, setting goals and working towards them, and seeking out resources and support as needed.

For example, an individual with autism may advocate for themselves in a workplace setting by communicating their needs and preferences to their employer or colleagues. They may also seek out resources and support, such as assistive technology or accommodations, to help them succeed in their job.

Overall, advocacy and self-advocacy are important for ensuring that individuals with autism have their needs and rights respected and supported. It is important for individuals with autism to have a strong support network that can help them advocate for their own needs and rights, as well as the needs and rights of others with autism.

# 7- Conclusion

- **Summary of key points**

Here is a summary of key points about autism, also known as autism spectrum disorder (ASD):

1. ASD is a complex neurodevelopmental disorder that affects communication and social interaction.

2. There is no cure for ASD, but there are a variety of treatments and interventions that can help individuals with ASD to manage their symptoms and to improve their communication and social skills.

3. The most effective treatments and interventions for ASD are typically tailored to the individual's needs and may involve a combination of therapies, medications, and other interventions.

4. The best treatment and intervention plan for ASD will depend on the individual's specific needs and circumstances, and it is important to work closely with a healthcare team to determine the most appropriate course of treatment.

5. There are a variety of strategies that can be helpful for managing daily life with ASD, including establishing a routine, using visual supports, encouraging independence, managing sensory issues, communicating clearly and consistently, and seeking support.

6. It is important to educate oneself about ASD and to work closely with a healthcare team to ensure that the individual receives the most appropriate treatment and support.

7. ASD is a spectrum disorder, which means that individuals with ASD may have a wide range of symptoms and severity.

8. Symptoms of ASD may include difficulty with communication and social interaction, repetitive behaviors, and sensitivity to sensory stimuli.

9. The cause of ASD is not fully understood, but research suggests that it may involve a combination of genetic and environmental factors.

10. Early diagnosis and intervention can be important for the treatment and management of ASD. It is important to seek a evaluation if there are concerns about the individual's development or behavior.

11. There is a wide range of treatments and interventions available for ASD, including behavioral therapies, medications, educational and support services, and alternative and complementary therapies.

12. It is important to work closely with a healthcare team to determine the most appropriate treatment and intervention plan for the individual.

13. It can be helpful to seek support from family, friends, and support groups to manage daily life with ASD.

14. It is important to educate oneself about ASD and to stay up-to-date on the latest research and treatment options.

- **Role Models and Inspiration**

There are many successful individuals who have autism and have made significant contributions in various fields. These success stories can serve as role models and provide inspiration for individuals with autism and their families. Here are a few examples:

1. Elon Musk: Elon Musk is a South African-born entrepreneur, inventor, and engineer. He is the founder, CEO, and lead designer of SpaceX, co-founder and CEO of Neuralink, and co-founder and CEO of Tesla, Inc. Musk has been open about his diagnosis of Asperger syndrome, a form of autism that affects social interaction and communication skills. Despite these challenges, he has become one of the most influential figures in modern technology, revolutionizing space exploration and transportation, and driving the adoption of electric vehicles.

2. Temple Grandin: Temple Grandin is an American professor of animal science at Colorado State University, consultant to the livestock industry on animal behavior, and autism activist. She was diagnosed with autism at the age of two and struggled with social interaction as a child. However, she also had a strong interest in animals and became a pioneer in the field of animal behavior, developing new methods for humane livestock handling. She has also become a leading advocate for people with autism, sharing her own experiences and promoting understanding and acceptance of neurodiversity.

3. Dan Aykroyd: The Canadian actor and comedian has been very open about his diagnosis with Asperger's syndrome, a form of autism. Despite his challenges, Aykroyd has had a successful career in comedy, acting, and music.

4. Susan Boyle: Susan Boyle is a Scottish singer who rose to fame after appearing on the TV show "Britain's Got Talent" in 2009. She was diagnosed with Asperger syndrome in 2012, but had already become a global sensation thanks to her powerful voice and inspiring story. Boyle's success demonstrates that people with autism can excel in

many different fields, and that their unique perspectives and talents can enrich the world in many ways.

5. Chris Packham: The British naturalist and television presenter has been very open about his diagnosis with Asperger's syndrome. He has hosted many popular wildlife programs and has also been involved in advocacy work for autism awareness.

6. Satoshi Tajiri: The creator of the wildly popular video game franchise Pokemon has Asperger's syndrome. Tajiri's interest in insect collecting as a child served as the inspiration for the game's concept.

7. Daryl Hannah: The American actress has been very open about her diagnosis with autism. Despite her challenges, she has had a successful career in film and has also been involved in activism for environmental and social causes.

8. Anthony Ianni: The former Michigan State University basketball player is a motivational speaker and autism advocate. He was the first Division I college basketball player to be diagnosed with autism and has been very open about his experiences.

These success stories demonstrate that individuals with autism can have fulfilling and successful lives in various fields. It is important for individuals with autism and their families to have positive role models and examples to look up to, and to understand that autism does not have to limit one's potential for success.

- **Encouragement for individuals with autism and their families**

To individuals with autism:

You are valued and loved for who you are, and you have unique strengths and abilities that make you special. It may be challenging at times to navigate the world with autism, but you are capable of achieving your goals and living a fulfilling life. You are not alone, and there are many resources and supports available to help you succeed. Remember to be kind to yourself and to celebrate your accomplishments, no matter how small they may seem. You have the potential to make a positive impact on the world, and you are capable of achieving great things.

To families of individuals with autism:

Caring for a loved one with autism can be a rewarding but also challenging experience. It is important to remember that you are not alone and that there are many resources and supports available to help you navigate this journey. It is also important to take care of yourself and to seek support from others when needed. Don't be afraid to ask for help, and don't be afraid to advocate for your loved one's needs. Remember to celebrate your loved one's accomplishments and to focus on their strengths. Most importantly, remember to show love and acceptance to your loved one, and to let them know that they are valued and loved for who they are.

# SPECIAL THANKS

I would like to extend a special thank you to the person who has read this book to the end. Thank you for taking the time to learn about autism and for showing an interest in this

important topic. I hope that you have found the information provided to be helpful and informative.

Understanding and supporting individuals with autism is an important task, and your willingness to learn about this topic is greatly appreciated. Thank you for your dedication to improving the lives of individuals with autism and for your commitment to creating a more inclusive and understanding world. Your efforts make a difference, and I hope that this book has helped to inspire and motivate you to continue making a positive impact. Thank you again for reading this book, and I wish you the best on your journey of learning and understanding.

Printed in Great Britain
by Amazon